PowerPhonics™

You Can Do It!

Learning the Y Sound

Janet Carson

The Rosen Publishing Group's
PowerKids Press™
New York

You can do many jobs when you grow up.

You can work on a farm.

You can grow yams and yellow beans.

yams

yellow beans

You can work as a bus driver.

You can drive a yellow bus.

SCHOOL BUS
EMERGENCY DOOR
80
STOP
IT'S UNLAWFUL TO PASS
WHEN RED LIGHT IS FLASHING

You can work in big yards.

You can grow yellow flowers.

You can work at a zoo.

You can feed yaks at the zoo.

Yes! You can do it!

Word List

yaks

yams

yards

yellow

yes

you

Instructional Guide

Note to Instructors:
One of the essential skills that enable a young child to read is the ability to associate letter-sound symbols and blend these sounds to form words. Phonics instruction can teach children a system that will help them decode unfamiliar words and, in turn, enhance their word-recognition skills. We offer a phonics-based series of books that are easy to read and understand. Each book pairs words and pictures that reinforce specific phonetic sounds in a logical sequence. Topics are based on curriculum goals appropriate for early readers in the areas of science, social studies, and health.

Letter/Sound: y – Have the child listen to the following sentences and tell which words begin with the same sound as *yes: Your mom's cookies taste yummy. The kids are yelling in the yard.* Continue with sentences using other initial **y** words, such as *yam, yo-yo, year, you, yak, yes, young,* etc. As the child responds, list the words on a chalkboard or dry-erase board. Have the child underline the initial **y** in each of them.
- Give a clue about a listed word and have the child name it. (Example: *I'm thinking of something good to eat that starts with* ***y***.) Continue with remaining words.

Phonics Activities: Have the child tell the vowel sound they hear in the word *yell.* Write *yell* on the chalkboard or dry-erase board. Have the child change the initial consonant to form other words, such as *bell, fell, tell, sell, Nell.* Continue with *yam* and *yap.*
- Write sentences that have a missing word on the chalkboard or dry-erase board. Provide three words that would make sense in each sentence. Ask the child to choose words that start with the initial **y** sound. For example: *Bob bought a __________ at the store.* (Possible responses: *ball, yo-yo, toy car.*) *I'll go first, Tom ___________(called, yelled, said).*
- Write the words *yo-yo* and *yum-yum.* Talk about how the words are alike. Add *yoo-hoo* to the list. Ask: "How is *yoo-hoo* like *yo-yo* and *yum-yum?*" "How is it different?" Introduce other hyphenated words *(tom-tom, go-go, boo-hoo)* as well as words having identical first and second syllables *(pompom, bonbon, tutu).*

Additional Resources:
- Flanagan, Alice K. *Riding the School Bus with Mrs. Kramer.* Danbury, CT: Children's Press, 1999.
- Fowler, Allan. *If It Weren't for Farmers.* Danbury, CT: Children's Press, 1993.

Published in 2002 by The Rosen Publishing Group, Inc.
29 East 21st Street, New York, NY 10010

Book Design: Haley Wilson

Photo Credits: Cover, p. 3 © Jim Cummins/FPG International; p. 5 © Digital Stock; p. 7 (top) © Jeff Dunn/Index Stock; p. 7 (bottom) © Inga Spence/Index Stock; p. 9 by Donna Scholl; p. 11 © Stephen Simpson/FPG International; p. 13 © David Young-Wolff/Photo Edit/PictureQuest; p. 15 © SuperStock; p. 17 © C. C. Lockwood/Animals Animals; p. 19 © Peter Weimann/Animals Animals; p. 21 © Jim Cummins/FPG International.

Library of Congress Cataloging-in-Publication Data

Carson, Janet.
You can do it! : learning the Y sound / Janet Carson.—1st ed.
p. cm. — (Power phonics/phonics for the real world)
ISBN 0-8239-5933-3 (lib. bdg.)
ISBN 0-8239-8278-5 (pbk)
6-pack ISBN 0-8239-9246-2
1. Occupations—Juvenile literature. 2. Reading—Phonetic method—Juvenile literature. [1. Occupations.] I. Title. II. Series.
HB2581 .C37 2002
331.7'02—dc21
2001000463

Manufactured in the United States of America